Economy and Industry in Ancient Rome

Daniel C. Gedacht

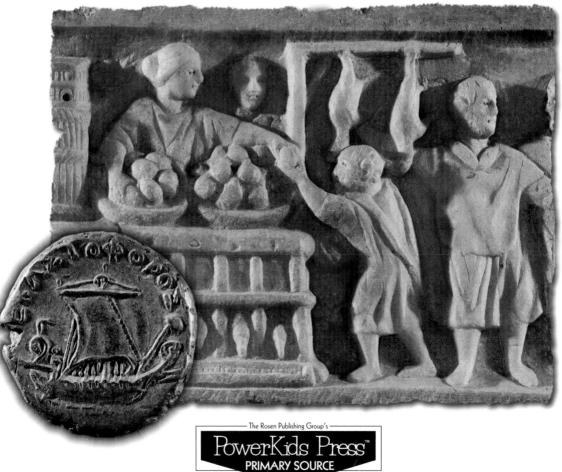

The Rosen Publishing Group's

PowerKids Press™
PRIMARY SOURCE

New York

For the Levys

Published in 2004 by The Rosen Publishing Group, Inc.
29 East 21st Street, New York, NY 10010

First Edition

Editor: Rachel O'Connor
Book Design: Michael J. Caroleo
Photo Researcher: Adriana Skura

Library of Congress Cataloging-in-Publication Data

Gedacht, Daniel C.
Economy and industry in ancient Rome / Daniel C. Gedacht.— 1st ed.
        v. cm.— (Primary sources of ancient civilizations. Rome)
Includes bibliographical references and index.
Contents: Work in ancient Rome—Farming and agriculture—Shops and markets—Milling and baking—Building and construction—Mining—Women in industry—Taxes—Foreign trade—Currency.
    ISBN 0-8239-6780-8 (library binding)—ISBN 0-8239-8946-1 (pbk.)
1. Rome—Economic conditions—Juvenile literature. 2. Industries—Rome—Juvenile literature. [1. Rome—Economic conditions. 2. Industries—Rome.] I. Title. II. Series.
    HC39 .G43 2004
    330.937'6—dc21
                                                                                        2003002332
Manufactured in the United States of America

Contents

Patricians often looked down on the working class of Rome. However, without the hardworking plebeians, such as the carpenter shown in this carving, Rome's economy would have been weak.

Work in Ancient Rome

In ancient Rome, people began their day at dawn. The labor was divided based on a person's social standing, or class. Upper-class men, called patricians, made money by receiving rent and taxes from the land they owned, so they spent their time on political activities or at leisure. The common citizens, called plebeians, and the slaves had to work. Some plebeians worked as farmers on the land they rented from a patrician. Others were craftsmen or merchants. Slaves did whatever work their masters ordered them to do, but many worked in the same jobs as did plebeians. The hardest jobs, such as mining and milling flour, often were given to the slaves.

◀ Top: *In this painting from the first century A.D., a peasant is leading a team of oxen as he goes about his agricultural duties.*

Farming and Agriculture

Roman civilization and its economy were based on agriculture. Many Romans throughout the empire worked as farmers, and food was the most important item for trade. By the second century B.C., the patricians owned most of the land, but they did not work it themselves. They rented the land to plebeians or got slaves to farm it. On their plots, the plebeians and the slaves would grow grains, fruits, and vegetables, including cabbages and turnips. They might also raise animals for milk, eggs, and meat. Plebeian farmers often grew more than they needed for their families and used the surplus to trade for other goods at markets, to pay taxes, and to pay rent to the landowners.

This mosaic shows farmers and hunters in scenes from country life in the Roman Empire in the third century A.D. The people who worked the land in ancient Rome rarely made much money, and the work was hard. ▶

This sculpture shows a Roman weighing produce at a market, while a scribe records the weight. Although the patricians generally did not shop themselves, the market areas were important places for them to go to talk about politics and current events.

Shops and Markets

The first Roman shops sprang up in the seventh century B.C., selling salt to flavor foods and to preserve meat. By the second century B.C., as the population grew, larger markets opened. One of the largest markets was the Roman Forum, near the Tiber River. The river gave the market access to the barges that brought goods into the city. There were other markets for cattle, fruits and vegetables, fish, and oil. Barbershops, shoemakers, and leather shops were usually found in poorer neighborhoods because these places were noisy and dirty. Patricians felt it was beneath them to go to these poorer markets. They sent their slaves to do the shopping.

◄ Bottom: *In this market scene from the second or third century A.D., a butcher is surrounded by his tools as he chops meat in his shop.*

Milling and Baking

In the early days of Rome, most people made their own bread from the grain they produced. However, by the first century A.D., Romans got most of their bread from bakeries. Also, Rome began to import grain from territories in its empire because Rome could not produce enough grain for its growing population. When the grain arrived off the merchant ships, it was transported to mills for processing. There were more than 200 mills in Rome by the second century A.D. The grain was made into flour by huge millstones, which were turned by either slaves or donkeys. The work was extremely hard. After it was ground, the flour was shipped to bakeries and baked into bread.

Most mills required manual labor, but some mills near the Tiber River used waterpower to turn the wheels. This is a grain mill from Pompeii, Italy. ▶

This wall painting from Naples, Italy, shows a baker at his stall selling fresh bread.

This sculpture of people making loaves of bread is from the coffin of a Roman baker, M. Virgilius Eurisace.

Building and Construction

Construction was another major business in ancient Rome. Apartments and houses were constantly going up. As the city grew, emperors ordered the construction of large baths, temples, and buildings to show the wealth and power of Rome and to keep the citizens happy. Barges brought wood, stone, and marble up the Tiber River nearly every day. Slaves worked at the many brick factories to produce even more materials. Slaves also provided the huge amount of workers necessary for the construction projects. Romans were excellent builders and many of their buildings, such as the Colosseum, exist today, thousands of years later.

◀ *Romans built large public bathhouses where people would go in the afternoon to wash, exercise, and relax. Pictured here is a tepidarium, or warm room, of a public bathhouse in the Roman countryside.*

Mining and Metalworking

Romans developed mining techniques to extract valuable and useful metals from the earth. The work, usually done by slaves, was hard and unsafe. After the metals were collected, craftsmen worked the iron and the bronze into the weapons and armor needed by the military. They also made pots and pans from copper and brass. In order to mold the metal, the ores that had been mined needed to be heated in an oven. The metals were heated to a liquid state and were poured into molds to cool into useful shapes. Later, stronger metals were heated and then were hammered into shape. Romans were known for their skilled metalwork and statues crafted from bronze and other metals.

This relief sculpture from the Museo della Civilita Romana shows a blacksmith hammering metal.

This bronze gladiator's helmet from the first century A.D. is an example of what the Romans made with the metals they mined.

15

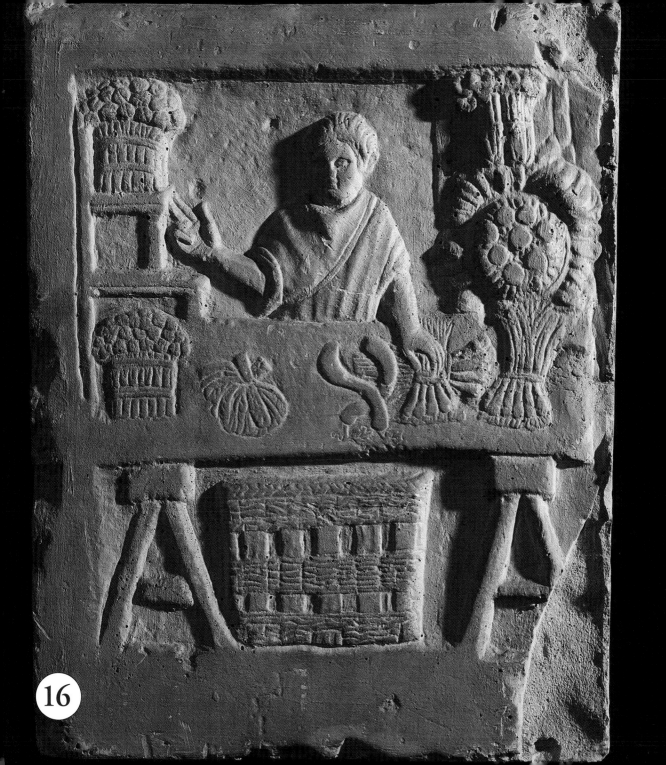

Women in Industry

Most women in ancient Rome married early and spent their lives raising a family and managing the home. They also managed the farm while their husbands were away or at war. They were responsible for finding people to work the land or for working it themselves with the help of their family. They also made sure taxes and rent were paid, and they traded goods at the market.

Some women worked outside the home to earn money. Women without husbands were often forced to take jobs so that they would not go hungry. Some women worked as dressmakers or tailors, making clothing for the wealthy men and women who lived nearby. A woman might also find work as a hairdresser.

◀ *In this relief sculpture, a woman is selling or trading goods at a market.* 17

Taxes

The Roman government developed a system of taxes and collected them throughout the empire. Tax collectors gathered taxes for each region. Some of these taxes were sent to Rome for construction projects and for the emperor's personal treasury.

In the country, plebeians either gave the tax collector a portion of the grain they grew or paid in money. In the cities, plebeians did not have to pay taxes. Instead, patricians contributed taxes that were used to pay for food for the poor. Under the Roman tax system, many tax officials took bribes. Bribes were so common that official bribery rates were printed and posted in every region.

In this sculpture, tax collectors gather around to count what they have received in grain or money from the taxpaying Roman citizens. ▶

Romans made coins from the silver they mined in Spain. This silver coin from 44 B.C. has a picture of Julius Caesar on one side.

This art from the third century A.D. shows a busy Roman harbor.

Trade

By the first century A.D., more than one million people lived in Rome. The empire stretched from England to North Africa, and from Spain to eastern Europe and Turkey. Food and building materials were traded throughout the empire, and merchants traveled as far as China to bring back spices and silk. The system of roads helped merchants to transport goods. Also, people used the same Roman coins throughout the empire, making the buying and selling of goods easier. By the fourth century A.D., Rome imported more than 400,000 tons (362,873.9 t) of grain each year. Ships often arrived at and left Rome's two main ports, Pozzuoli and Ostia.

◀ Top: *Merchant ships carried grain from Egypt, wine from Spain and France, marble and stone from northern Italy, and fish from North Africa.*

21

Currency

Early Romans had little need of money because they grew or produced almost everything they needed themselves. As the empire grew, however, the government minted metal money, which came into common use. In the second century B.C., Romans began using a bronze coin called the as, among others. These were replaced by silver coins, called denarius, after Rome captured large silver mines in Spain in the first century B.C. When Augustus became emperor in 31 B.C., he minted the gold aureus. As coins became available, it was easier for the empire to collect taxes. It was also easier for people to buy and sell goods throughout the empire. Currency helped to strengthen Rome's economy.

Glossary

access (AK-ses) A way to get somewhere easily.

barges (BARJ-ez) Boats with flat bottoms, used to carry goods on rivers.

blacksmith (BLAK-smith) A person who makes and fixes iron objects.

bribes (BRYBZ) Money or favors given in return for something else.

coffin (KAH-fin) A box that holds a dead body.

craftsmen (KRAFTS-men) Workmen who practice a certain trade.

developed (dih-VEH-lupt) Worked out in great detail.

extract (ek-STRAKT) To take one item out of another.

gladiator (GLA-dee-ay-tur) A person who fought to the death against other people or animals.

import (IM-port) To bring in from another country.

industry (IN-dus-tree) A moneymaking business in which many people work and make money producing a particular product.

leisure (LEE-zhur) Time to do whatever one wants.

manual (MAN-yuh-wul) By hand.

materials (muh-TEER-ee-ulz) What things are made of.

millstones (MIL-stohnz) Heavy, circular stones used for making grain into a powder.

minted (MINT-ed) Made into money.

mosaic (moh-ZAY-ik) A picture made by fitting together small pieces of stone, glass, or tile and sticking them in place.

ores (ORZ) Rocks that contain metal.

scribe (SKRYB) A person whose job is to copy books by hand.

surplus (SUR-plus) More than enough.

transported (TRANZ-port-ed) Moved things from one place to another.

Index

Primary Sources

Cover. Market scene. Roman funerary stele. Third century A.D. Museo Ostiense, Ostia, Italy. **Inset.** Bronze coin. Navigator at the stern. Mint of Alexandria, Egypt. Period of the Roman emperor Nero. (A.D. 54–68) **Page 4. Top.** Peasant with a team of oxen. Fragment from the fresco from Caseggiato di Serapide, Ostia, Italy. **Bottom.** Funerary stele of Pubio Longidieno, the carpenter of the fleet. The deceased is shown constructing a boat with an ax. First century B.C. Museo Nazionale, Ravenna, Italy. **Page 7.** Scenes from rural life, showing shepherds, a bird hunter, and a tiger hunt. Detail of a Roman mosaic from the House of Icarius at Oudna, Tunisia. Third century, A.D. **Page 8. Bottom.** A butcher working in his shop. Second to third centuries A.D. Museo Ostiense, Ostia, Italy. **Page 11. Left.** A baker at his stall offers fresh bread to customers. Wall painting from the Casa del Panettiere, Pompeii, Italy. The city of Pompeii was buried by Mount Vesuvius in A.D. 79. **Page 15. Top.** A blacksmith hammering metal. Stele relief. First century A.D. **Bottom.** Gladiator's helmet. Bronze. First century A.D. **Page 19. Top.** Silver denarius with the portrait of Julius Caesar on one side. 44 B.C. **Bottom.** Tax collection scene. Roman relief from a funeral stele. Second to third centuries A.D. **Page 20. Bottom.** Roman harbor, with buildings and temple. Glass opus sectile work. Third century A.D.

Web Sites

Due to the changing nature of Internet links, PowerKids Press has developed an online list of Web sites related to the subject of this book. This site is updated regularly. Please use this link to access the list:

www.powerkidslinks.com/psaciv/econrom/